Teach Yourself to Read Music
A Guide for Pop, Rock, Blues and Jazz Singers

By Jeffrey Deutsch

W9-CKQ-598

Table of Contents

ISBN 0-7935-9421-9

Houston
PUBLISHING, INC.

EXCLUSIVELY DISTRIBUTED BY

HAL•LEONARD®
CORPORATION
7777 W. BLUEMOUND RD. P.O. BOX 13819 MILWAUKEE, WI 53213

Visit Hal Leonard Online at
www.halleonard.com

ABOUT THE AUTHOR

Jeffrey Deutsch has taught sightsinging for over fifteen years, including classes, workshops, and individual lessons at Elmhurst College in Elmhurst, Illinois, and the Center for Voice in Chicago. In addition, he is a very busy singer/pianist, entertaining on cruise ships, in hotel and restaurant piano bars, and with jazz big bands. He has performed his one-man show "The Great American Songbook" to appreciative audiences throughout the Midwest, and is often joined on gigs by his wife, Vivian Davis.

ALSO BY JEFFREY DEUTSCH

Musicianship for Singers: What Singers Need to Learn About Music that Instrumentalists Already Know is the how-to book that helps singers catch up with instrumentalists in musical knowledge and skill. It has sections on chartwriting, piano accompaniment, sightsinging, transposing, harmonizing and other practical skills that singers need in the studio and on the bandstand. This "singer-friendly" book comes with a CD and contains many examples and exercises.

DEDICATION

To Robert Bowker, who has helped, taught and inspired me and many others, in many ways.

INTRODUCTION

The way the music business is today, singers need to know how to sight sing. We are continually handed music in the recording studio and in rehearsals for stage shows, and we are expected to read it the way most instrumentalists can. Unfortunately, most singers haven't received the training they need to read music. They never learned to read any kind of music, especially not modern pop music. Either they didn't take courses in sight singing or they learned very little when they did. This leaves them forever dependent on instrumentalists to play their parts for them, hoping their own ears will remember what was played. Because of this sight singing deficiency, many singers fake it. They pretend to be sight singing when in actuality, the written music is of no use to them.

I faked it for a long time, always afraid I'd get caught and feeling guilty that I didn't know how to read, even though I'd been a singer all my life. Then I realized there is no reason to feel guilty for something you haven't been taught. Just because you can speak a language (that is, sing) doesn't mean you understand it (that is, read). The two skills are different. You have to learn to sight sing. After I learned to sight sing an amazing feeling of calm and confidence came over me. The first time I was handed a piece of music in the studio, I said to myself, "Yes, I can sing this!", and it was like coming up from under water and taking a big breath of fresh air.

This book presents a system for learning the grammar of music - the rules by which it is understood. Music must make "sense". It usually follows rules that make it sound "right" to our ears. Throughout our lives we have developed instincts about music based on these rules, whether we know it or not. But if we rely on these instincts alone, we wind up making mistakes by singing what makes sense to us or what we hear in our head, rather than what is actually written on the page. The two may not be the same. The system presented in this book will keep you focused on the page and not on the "melody maker" in your head.

This book starts slowly with the basics of sight singing and adds more complicated elements one by one. It uses visual images to help you hear in your head what you see on the page. Each chapter has a review of basic, practical music theory. Unlike most other sight singing books, it is specially geared to the singer of pop music. It concentrates on singing in the treble clef rather than the other clefs. Most of the exercises are in 4-4 or cut-time rather than in more exotic time signatures. The exercises are in the more often used keys for singers. Once you learn the system in these keys you can sight sing in any given key. The book also stresses modern syncopation, the most difficult part of sight singing for most singers and a subject not addressed in many books.

There are sight singing examples and exercises used in each chapter, and they are highlighted at the end of each chapter. In each chapter one will find an original song that is similar to music that the professional singer will be asked to sight sing. The accompanying CD will help you to monitor your efforts. You can practice singing the song in each chapter without the recorded vocal example (turn off one of the channels), and then use the recorded vocal example to check yourself (turn the channel on again).

For further help I suggest using my book, "Musicianship For Singers", which not only has more exercises for sight singing, but also has more examples and exercises to help you with the system that underlies sight singing.

Give yourself time to learn to sight sing. It doesn't happen overnight. It takes a lot of practice, somewhat like becoming fluent in a new language. There is nothing like acquiring the confidence in a skill that will not only help you to get work more easily, but also make you feel more at ease while participating in the world of professional singing.

CHAPTER ONE
C MAJOR DIATONIC SCALE, LETTER NAMES AND NUMBERS

Every song that we are asked to sightsing is in a particular key. That means that the notes that make up the melody of the song will, for the most part, be in a particular scale: the diatonic scale that starts on the key note. So if a song is in C Major, its key note is C and the notes in its melody will mostly be in the C Major diatonic scale.

You probably know this scale already, because you learned it in kindergarten. Listen to the CD, 1-1* (all numbers with * after them will be on the CD). Now sing along with 1-1* several times, on "la-la-la".

That's the C Major diatonic scale. Each of the notes in that scale has a letter name. They are, in order:

C D E F G A B C again.

Notice that there are no sharps (#) or flats (b) in this key. Sing along with 1-1* several more times, only using the letter names this time.

Now, sing along with 1-1* several more times, using the numbers 1 through 8.

Now, play this scale on the piano (or any keyboard). Start with the white key below the pair of black keys in the middle of the keyboard. This key is called middle C. Play eight white notes in a row. Sound familiar?

You just played this:

1-2

If you started at the eighth note (C again) and played eight more white notes in a row, you'd have the C Major diatonic scale again, only higher in pitch. If you started on any other C and played eight white notes in a row, you'd always have the C Major diatonic scale.

So you have notes that you sing (on la-la-la, letters or numbers) and the same notes to play on the piano. But the song you have to sing is written on paper. How do you translate what's on the paper to your voice? How do you sing the correct <u>pitches?</u>

TREBLE CLEF AND LEDGER LINES

The pitches the composer wants us to sing are written on a staff with a clef symbol at its left edge:

1-3

The clef symbol tells us which pitches (letter names) are assigned to the lines and spaces of the staff. The treble clef (above), which we use the most often for melodies, tells us that the bottom line of the staff is the E above middle C on the piano, the next line up is G, then B, then D, and the top line is F. The spaces between the lines are (from bottom to top) F, A, C and E. Singing up and down the staff is like walking up and down stairs. The diatonic scale from 1 to 8 is like a staircase from the floor to the ceiling.

1-4

E   G   B   D   F   F   A   C   E

Because we can sing higher and lower than these pitches, we can add little lines, called ledger lines, above and below the staff:

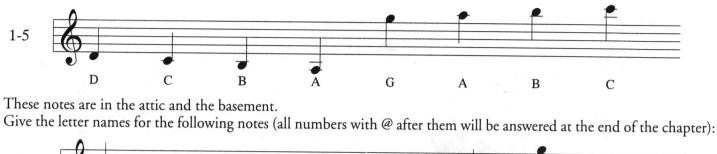

1-5

D   C   B   A   G   A   B   C

These notes are in the attic and the basement.

Give the letter names for the following notes (all numbers with @ after them will be answered at the end of the chapter):

1-6@

So the C Major diatonic scale that we now know so well begins on the first ledger line below the staff with the treble clef on it, and goes up seven more notes. Sing along on numbers, then on letters, while looking at the notes on the staff:

1-7*

C   D   E   F   G   A   B   C

Other clefs will designate different notes, but we won't need to learn them in this book. Later on, we'll learn four other keys. But for now, we'll just be using C Major.

6

Sing the following exercises, first along with the CD, and then by yourself. (And turn off the "melody-maker" in your head, the musician who convinces you that you can stop reading the notes because you know exactly where each exercise is going. That's how you wind up singing wrong notes. Don't just sing - keep reading.)

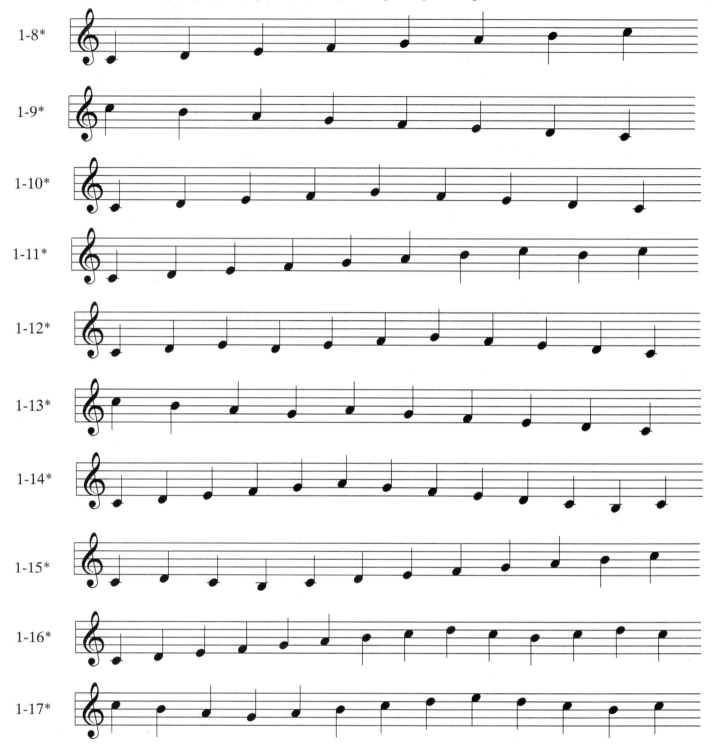

Congratulations! You can sightsing. If all music was this simple, you could stop right now. But things will get a little more complicated.

Sing the following exercises, just on numbers. Pick a low note in your register, call that "1", and sing up and down the scale.

1-18
1) 1 2 3 4 5 6 7 8 7 6 5 4 3 2 1

2) 8 7 6 5 4 3 2 1 2 3 4 5 6 7 8

3) 1 2 3 4 3 4 5 6 5 6 7 8
       7 6 5 4 5 4 3 2 3 2 1

4) 8 7 6 5 6 5 4 3 4 3 2 1

5) 1 2 3 2 3 4 3 4 5 4 5 6
       5 6 7 6 7 8 7 6 5 4 3 2 1

You now know the pitches of the notes on the staff. But when do you sing each note? And how long do you hold it? That's rhythm.

4/4 OR COMMON TIME

Right next to the clef, there's a fraction, called the time signature. The one we'll see most often is 4/4. It's so common, in fact, that it's called "Common Time" and abbreviated with a big "C":

1-19

This is what 4/4, or C, means: for every measure (the space between two vertical lines, called "bar lines"), four evenly-spaced beats will go by, and they will each be equal to a quarter-note:

1-20

1   2   3   4   1   2   3   4   1   2   3   4   1   2   3   4

NOTE AND REST VALUES

Each of the notes in 1-20 is a quarter-note, and so there are four of them in every measure of 4/4. But if music only had quarter-notes, it would be very boring. So there are other notes, too:

1-21

Whole   Half   Quarter   Eighth

Any combination of notes that equals four quarter-notes will fill up a measure of 4/4. Imagine that each measure costs a dollar, and you can pay for it with a dollar bill (whole note), two half dollars (half notes) or four quarters (quarter notes). For instance, these measures all have the correct amount of notes in them:

1-22

These measures don't:

1-23

In the following measures, which have the correct amount of notes, which have too many, and which have too few?

1-24@

So in 4/4, the top number tells us that there are four even beats in each measure, and the bottom number tells us that each beat equals a quarter-note. So four quarter-notes worth of music will go by in every measure. You can count along:

1-25*

Notice that when notes smaller than quarter-notes are used, we have to subdivide the beat and use symbols (like "&") as well as numbers.

Count along with the following exercises on the CD:

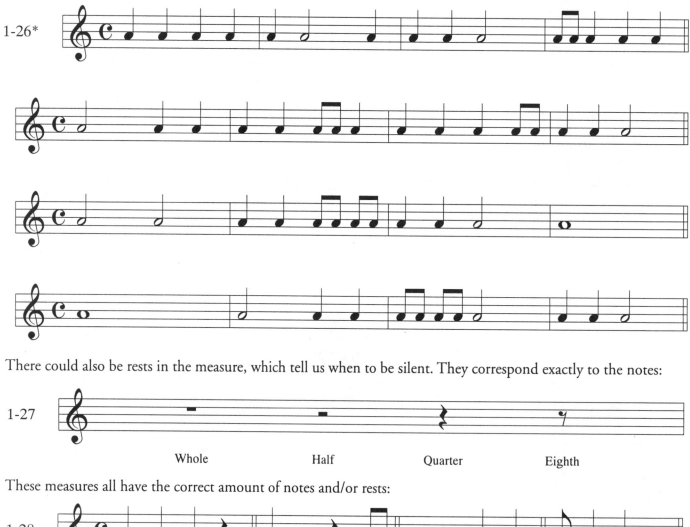

There could also be rests in the measure, which tell us when to be silent. They correspond exactly to the notes:

1-27

Whole   Half   Quarter   Eighth

These measures all have the correct amount of notes and/or rests:

These don't:

1-29

Which of these have the correct amount, which have too many, and which have too few?

1-30@

EXAMPLES

Sing each of the following examples along with the CD at least two times, once with numbers, once with letters or once on "la-la la":

10
EXERCISES

Now sing the following exercises which are not on the CD. Again, sing them at least two different ways. If you have trouble, go to the Appendix. And make sure you turn off your "melody-maker".

11

12

SONG 1*

Finally, here is a simple song for you to sightsing. Give yourself a C on the piano, sing the diatonic scale until it's firmly in your head, and then start by just singing the melody on "la-la-la". If you can't get the correct pitches and the correct rhythms at the same time, keep working on the pitches until you're sure of them, and then go back and get the rhythms right. Finally, put the lyrics into the song, and listen to the CD to see if you got it right.

Simple ballad

ANSWERS

ASSIGNMENT

Check out a book of children's songs from the library, and sightsing through it.

CHAPTER TWO
G MAJOR AND F MAJOR DIATONIC SCALES

There is a major diatonic scale for each of the twelve different notes on the piano. They all sound the same, because the distances between the notes are always the same, and that way we hear the entire scale that's so familiar to us. It's like the same set of stairs in a different house.

But if you try to play another diatonic scale on the piano, say for instance G Major, you might start on a G, play up seven more white notes, and something would sound wrong. Play the following notes:

Do you hear what's wrong? In order for this to have the sound of the diatonic scale, one of the notes has to be changed. It's the F. It has to be raised to F# (the black note between F and G), or the scale won't be diatonic, it won't sound right. Imagine kicking the F out of the scale, and replacing it with F#.

Now we're in the key of G Major. Sing this scale.

KEY SIGNATURES

Rather than put a "#" in front of every F note in the melody of a song in G Major (there will probably be a lot of them), we put a "#" on the top line of the staff right after the clef.

This is a key signature. It says we're in the key of G Major, which means we'll mostly be using all the white notes except for F. From now on it's F#. Every time we see a note on the top line of the staff (high F) or the bottom space of the staff (low F), or any ledger line F, it'll be F#.

The key signature tells us what key we're in, and what notes are in the diatonic scale of that key.

Here's another one:

This is the key of F Major. Start with an F, play seven more white notes, and you'll hear another scale that's almost diatonic. One note has to be changed. It's the B. Lower it to a Bb (the black note between A and B), and the scale will be diatonic, and familiar.

Again, if we put that Bb in the key signature, we'll know to sing Bb every time a note appears on a line or space that we formerly called "B". This will happen a lot in the key of F Major. Sing this scale.

Remember, the key of C Major has no sharps or flats (black notes) in it, so there aren't any sharps or flats in the key signature after the clef when we're in C Major. All the other keys have at least one sharp or one flat in them, and they'll appear in the key signature after the clef. There will never be a sharp and a flat in the same key signature.

Just because the notes in the keys of G Major and F Major are a little different from the notes in C Major, there's no reason to worry. They will sound familiar. But the numbers shift over for each new key. In G Major, G is 1, of course. In F Major, F is 1. Same stairs, different house.

SHARPS, FLATS AND ENHARMONIC EQUIVALENTS

Did you notice that the black notes between the white notes have two different names, one sharp and one flat? The black note between C and D can be called either C# or Db. The black note between G and A can be called either G# or Ab. These pairs of notes are called "enharmonic equivalents" - they have two different names but they sound the same. Which one of the pair we choose to call a black note will usually be determined by what key we're in. Usually, if a black note is in a sharp key, we'll use its sharp name, not its flat one. And vice versa.

Give the enharmonic equivalent for each note:

NUMBER CHARACTERS, BELLS AND GONGS

My system of sightsinging uses numbers, because we use numbers all the time in our daily lives, and we already know that 6 is higher than 4, and so on. Also, numbers have practical applications when working with instrumentalists, who use numbers for everything. Practical music theory is based on numbers. The Nashville System of Notation, used in some of the best studios in the country, is all numbers.

But we can't just go up and down the scale, like we did in Chapter One. Melodies are more complicated than that, thankfully.

How do we go from one note in the scale to another that isn't right next to it?

If we get to know the sound of each number, its "character", its "personality", then all we need to do to sightsing is recognize what number is next, and sing the "character" of that number. No matter what key we're in, no matter what letter names the notes have, 1 will always sound like 1.

Let's go back to the key of C Major, and get to know the "character" of each number.

1 - The root of the scale, the note upon which the rest of the scale is built, the most important note, the note on which many melodies end, the note you must be able to hear in a windstorm, like a huge bell:

Get to know the sound of 1 very well. Whatever key you're in, it should always sound like a big bell at the bottom of the scale. Sing it.

Then there's 8, or the next "1" up, an interval of an octave away from 1. 8 has the same letter name as 1, so it will sound familiar (it's the root of the same diatonic scale, only starting higher). If you play both 1 and 8 at the same time on the piano, you almost can't tell that you're playing two different notes, they sound so similar in a way. 8 is another bell, a little smaller than 1, farther off in the distance:

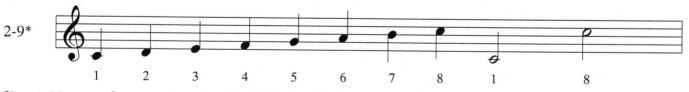

Sing 8. Now see if you can sing 1 again. Big bell at the bottom of the scale. Now 8 again. Smaller bell at the top of the scale. Go back and forth until you can find them easily.

Now, if you have to sightsing the following notes, you can do it:

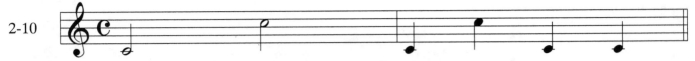

2-10

Now let's listen for 5. 5 is another bell, smaller than 1, larger than 8, right in the middle of the scale. It's the strong note half-way through the scale that signals a good resting place.

2-11*

1   2   3   4   5   1   5

Sing it.
Now sing the following notes (don't worry about rhythm):

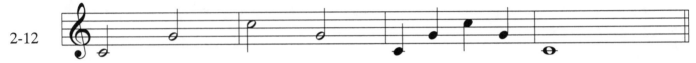

2-12

The last bell is 3. It's small, but very important; it's the note that determines whether a scale is Major or minor (we'll get to minor keys in Chapter Four). It gives the scale its "color". 3 is the sweet, happy, tiny bell between 1 and 5:

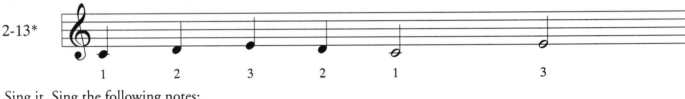

2-13*

1   2   3   2   1   3

Sing it. Sing the following notes:

2-14

So the bells in any key are the 1s, 3s, 5s and 8s of the diatonic scale in that key. Always know what lines and spaces the bells are on in the key you're using. If you can sing up and down the scale, and sing any bell at any time, you've got a great start on sightsinging.

What's left? For this chapter, it's just finding 2, 4, 6 and 7, the "gongs". These are harder to find than the bells, but they have distinctive characters all their own. Until we hear their individual sounds, we may need to silently sing the closest bell and then move up or down to the gong that we're trying to find. For instance, 7 is right below 8. If you need to sing 1 to 7, try ghost-singing 1 (8) 7.

7 has so much character that it has a name: leading tone. Since it's only a half-step away from 8, that bell that we hear so well at the top of the scale, it easily leads right up to it. We might be tempted to sing 8 when we should be singing 7. Often, the note after 7 is 8. That sounds "right" to our ears, because we hear it in practically every song in every style of music:

2-15*

8   7   8   7   8   7

Sing it. We might want to think of 7 as that weak note at the top of the scale that gives in to (resolves to) 8.

Similarly, 4 is only a half-step from 3, the important bell above 1. 4 is the note that we might sing on the "Ah-" of "A-men" after a hymn. It's suspended for a while, but it will almost always fall down to, give in to, resolve to its important neighbor, the bell 3.

2-16*

1   2   3   4   3   4   3   4

Sing it.

2 is right above 1. It's the first step we take away from 1, almost as if you were trying to decide whether to journey on to 3 and 4, or go back to 1:

2-17*   1   2   1   2   1   2   3   2   1   2

Sing it.

And finally, 6. 6 is in the no-man's land between 5 and 8.

Because it's hard to find, I think of 6 as being an independent kind of note, maybe even rebellious. And it's joyous, too. It's the note we hear tacked on to the final chord in a lot of barbershop quartet arrangements, happy and decisive:

2-18*   1   2   3   4   5   6   5   6

Sing it.

So there are the eight notes of the scale: the biggest bell 1, the farther bell 8, the big bell in the middle of the scale 5, the small color bell 3, the leading tone gong 7, the Amen gong 4, the tentative first step gong 2, and the gong in no-man's land 6. Of course, you can make up your own analogy, your own characters for these notes. But know what each one sounds like to you, so that when you see it on the staff you can say to yourself, "Ah, that's 5, I know what 5 sounds like," and the sound of 5 will pop into your head.

Put numbers under the following notes:

2-19@

Sing the following numbers in any key. Pick a low note and call it "1".

2-20   1) 1 2 1 3 1 4 1 5 1 6 1 7 1 8

2) 8 7 8 6 8 5 8 4 8 3 8 2 8 1

3) 1 3 2 4 3 5 4 6 5 7 6 8

4) 8 6 7 5 6 4 5 3 4 2 3 1

5) 1 3 5 1 5 1   2 4 6 2 6 2
   3 5 7 3 7 3   4 6 8 4 8 4
                5 3 1 5 1

6) 1 4 1 2 5 2 3 6 3   5 8 5

7) 1 4 2 5 3 6   5 8

20

CUT TIME

The other most often seen time signature besides 4/4 is cut time, abbreviated:

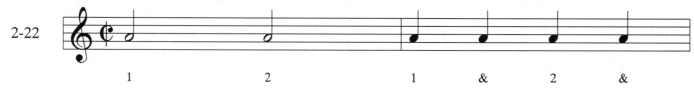

This is a term in music that different musicians explain in different ways. Here's what you need to know about cut time for sightsinging: it's written exactly like 4/4 (four quarter-notes worth of music in every measure), it's read exactly like 4/4, but it's felt differently. It's actually felt like 2/2: two half-notes per measure, each one getting a pulse, and the quarter-note now divides the beat, like the eighth-note did in 4/4:

Why do we have cut time, if it's so much like 4/4?   1) If the tempo is very fast, it's too difficult to snap along with four beats in every measure, so we "abbreviate" 4/4 by putting the music in cut time. Then, it's easier to snap along.   2) When the tempo is slow, an accompaniment in cut time will be more spacious than one in 4/4, which could make a ballad sound like a march.

Read cut time just like 4/4, but listen for a different feel in the accompaniment. And remember that when we're counting along with cut time, we only count to two in each measure.

Count along with the following exercises:

DOTTED NOTES

Music uses dots to extend the length of a note by one-half of its value:

Which of the following measures have too many or too few notes or rests in them?

Count along with the following:

When counting sixteenth-notes (there are two in every eighth note, four in every quarter-note), use "e" and "a":

Then singing a dotted eighth-note sixteenth-note pattern will sound like this:

Sing along with the following exercises:

22
EXAMPLES
Sing each of the following examples along with the CD.

EXERCISES

Sing the following exercises. Turn off your "melody-maker".

SONG 2*

Here's another song for you to sing. Melody first, then rhythms, then lyrics. Then check your efforts with the CD.

Moderately

ANSWERS

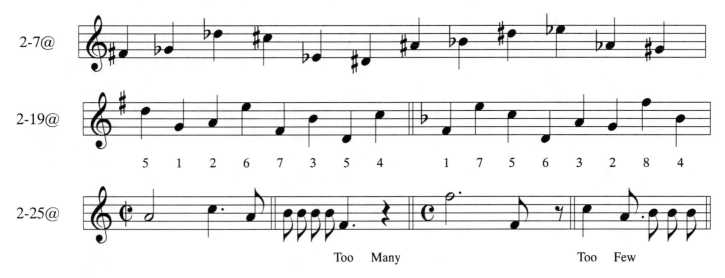

2-7@

2-19@

```
5  1  2  6  7  3  5  4    1  7  5  6  3  2  8  4
```

2-25@

Too   Many   Too   Few

ASSIGNMENT

Find a collection of Rodgers and Hart songs in the library, or buy one. Sing through as many songs as you can.

CHAPTER THREE
Bb MAJOR AND Eb MAJOR DIATONIC SCALES

The two other most important keys are Bb Major and Eb Major. Bb Major has two flats in its key signature, and therefore two black notes in its diatonic scale - Bb and Eb:

Eb Major has three flats - Bb, Eb and Ab:

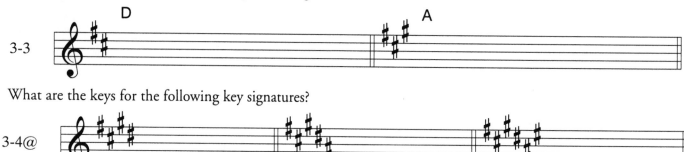

Play and sing these two new scales. Sound familiar? Make sure you work hard on Eb Major. A lot of sheet music is in Eb Major, because it's a good key for most men to sing in, and a lot of women, too. It fits a lot of people's ranges.

OTHER KEY SIGNATURES

You may need to sing in other keys besides C, F, G, Bb and Eb (though rarely). If so, just go about it the usual way: figure out which key you're in, find the key note on the piano, think of that note as 1 of the key, sing the diatonic scale, and set up your numbers from there. When in doubt, check the Appendix.

Here are the two formulas for figuring out what key we're in from the key signatures:

1) Sharp keys: go up a step from the last sharp on the right:

What are the keys for the following key signatures?

3-4@

2) Flat keys: go to the second-to-last flat on the right:

What are the keys for the following key signatures?

3-6@

The exception, of course, is the key of F Major, which we've already had. Since there is no second-to-last flat, we just have to memorize this one ("1 b: F as in "Jeff").

ACCIDENTALS, HALF-STEPS AND HORNS

Now you know all the notes in the five most commonly used diatonic scales. But there are twelve different notes (letter names) on the piano. If any scale only uses seven of them (and then repeats one at the top), what about the other five? Don't they ever get used?

Of course they do. They're called "accidentals" and they are part of what makes music interesting and exciting.

An accidental is any note that's not in the diatonic scale of the key we're in. It's easy to see what the accidentals are in the key of C Major. Since it only has the white notes in the scale, all five of the black notes (#s and bs) are accidentals. In G Major, however, F# is in the scale, so F is now an accidental. Similarly, in F Major, Bb is in the scale, so B is an accidental.

There can only be one version, sharp, flat or natural, of each letter in any scale. If there's a Bb in the scale, there can't be a B. If there's a D, there can't be a D#.

What are the five accidentals in the following keys?

3-7@   Bb _____ _____ _____ _____ _____
         Eb _____ _____ _____ _____ _____
         D _____ _____ _____ _____ _____
         A _____ _____ _____ _____ _____

You've spent a lot of time and effort learning to hear the notes of each major diatonic scale, and that's good, because you'll sing those notes more often than you'll sing accidentals. But how do you hear and sing the accidentals when you need to? There are two ways.

1) First of all, each accidental is a half-step above a note in the scale that you can hear, and a half-step below another note in the scale that you can hear. If you can't hear the accidental, ghost-sing one of the notes next to it, and then slide up or down a half-step to the accidental. For instance, in C Major, F# (that is, #4) is right above F (4), and right below G (5).

Since G is a bell in C Major, it will probably be easier to go to G first rather than F.
In G Major, F (b7) is between E (6) and F# (7). Ghost-sing F#, and then go down a half-step.

Half-steps are the smallest interval we are likely to ever sing. Sing these pairs of notes that are a half-step apart, along with the CD:

2) But second of all, it would be easier to sing the accidentals if we could just hear them, like we now hear the notes in the scale. If we assign a character to each of them, a particular quality, maybe even a color, they'll start to sound in our heads like the bells and gongs do. Perhaps they're horns.

There's #1/b2, the note in any scale between 1 and 2. In C Major, it's C#/Db. What is it in:

3-11@   G _____   F _____   Bb _____   Eb _____

This is a note that's sometimes used for comic effect. Think of it as the tricky, surprising note.

Sing it.

Then there's #2/b3, the note in any scale between 2 and 3. In C Major, it's D#/Eb. What is it in:

3-13@   G _____   F _____   Bb _____   Eb _____

This is the note that makes a minor scale minor (more about minor scales in Chapter Four). Think of it as the sad, poignant note.

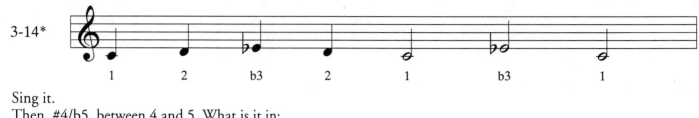

Sing it.

Then, #4/b5, between 4 and 5. What is it in:

3-15@   C _____   G _____   F _____   Bb _____   Eb _____

This is a note that's often used in horror movie soundtracks, and macabre TV show background music. Think of it as the eerie, suspenseful note.

Sing it.

Then, #5/b6, between 5 and 6. What is it in:

3-17@   C _____   G _____   F _____   Eb _____   D _____

This is a note that many composers of classical music have featured in their orchestral work. Think of it as the grand, noble note.

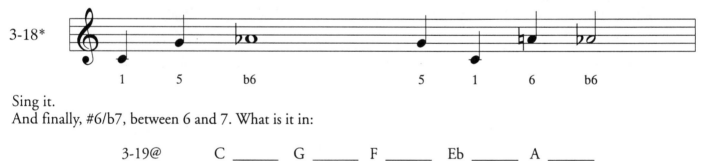

Sing it.

And finally, #6/b7, between 6 and 7. What is it in:

3-19@   C _____   G _____   F _____   Eb _____   A _____

This is one of the blue notes of jazz, rock and blues (more about blue notes in Chapter Five). Think of it as the wild, brassy note.

Sing it.

Again, you can make up your own ways of hearing the "characters" of these accidentals.

Here are some exercises to help you hear accidentals in any key. Pick any note, without going to the paino, and don't try to figure out what key you're in. Just sing numbers in a scale.

3-21*	1)	1	2	3	4	5	#4	5	6	5	4	3	2	1				
	2)	1	2	3	4	5	#4	5	4	3	#4	5	4	3	2	1		
	3)	8	7	6	5	6	b7	8	b7	6	5	6	7	8				
	4)	1	2	3	4	5	6	7	8	b7	6	5	6	b7	8	7	8	
	5)	1	2	3	2	b3	2	3	4	5	4	3	2	b3	2	1		
	6)	5	4	3	4	5	4	b3	4	5	4	3	2	1	2	b3	2	1
	7)	1	#1	2	#1	1	2	3	2	1	#1	2	#1	1				
	8)	5	6	7	6	5	b6	6	b6	5	6	7	8	7	6	b6	5	
	9)	1	#1	2	#2	3	4	#4	5	#5	6	#6	7	8				
	10)	8	7	b7	6	b6	5	b5	4	3	b3	2	b2	1				

Remember that every accidental has two names, one sharp and the other flat.

Important note: once a note is accidentalized in a measure, it stays that way for the entire measure. Then the next bar line cancels that accidental. If the composer wants to continue to use the accidental in the next measure, she has to repeat it in that second measure, and so on. So:

Sometimes the composer will want to remind you that an accidental in one measure has been cancelled by the bar line. She will put a "courtesy accidental" in the next bar. I always like to put parentheses around this courtesy accidental, as if to say: "I know you know this is supposed to be F, not F# any more, but here's a little reminder..."

3/4 TIME

You may sightsing some music in 3/4, though not as much as in 4/4 or cut time. 3/4 is waltz time. Count it like this:

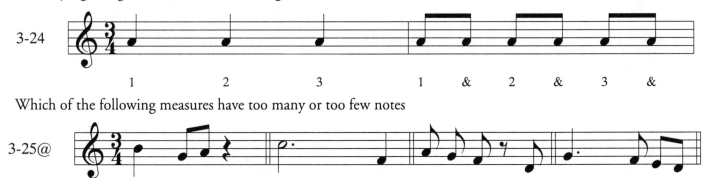

Which of the following measures have too many or too few notes

Sing the following rhythms on any pitch:

TIES

Ties are used to hold a note over a bar line:

or to hold a note within a measure when there's no other good way of writing it:

This musical phrase could also be written like this:

But technically, this isn't correct. We'll get back to this when we start singing syncopation in Chapter Four.

When singing ties, sing along normally, but don't sing the number of the second note that's attached to the first one by the tie:

Just hold the first note until the second note is finished. Keep the metronome in your head going. Don't stop it because you're holding out a note.

Sing the following rhythms on any pitch:

Note: don't confuse ties (lines from one note to another on the same line or space) with slurs, which are dynamic markings that link many different notes. Slurs tell us to make a single phrase out of those many notes.

PICK-UP NOTES

Sometimes a melody doesn't start right on or right after the downbeat (the first note of a measure). If there are notes before the start of a section of music, they're called "pick-up notes". They give us a kind of running start to the melody. For instance, the first three notes in this melody are pick-up notes:

Think of the first part of the melody to "Don't Get Around Much Anymore", or "It Had To Be You".
Count pick-up notes as if they're the last part of a full measure before the downbeat:

Sing the following rhythms on any note:

36
EXAMPLES

Sing along with the CD:

37

EXERCISES

Sing the following exercises without the CD (turn off the "melody-maker"):

40

SONG 3*

Here's another song for you to sightsing. Again, sightsing it first, then sing along with the accompaniment on the CD, and then listen to the vocal version on the CD to see how you did.

ANSWERS

3-4@

3-6@

3-7@
Bb:	B	C#	E	F#	G#
Eb:	E	F#	A	B	C#
D:	Eb	F	Ab	Bb	C
A:	Bb	C	Db	Eb	F

3-11@ G: G#/Ab F: F#/Gb Bb: B/Cb Eb: E/Fb

3-13@ G: A#/Bb F: G#/Ab Bb: C#/Db Eb: F#/Gb

3-15@ C: F#/Gb G: C#/Db F: B/Cb Bb: E/Fb Eb: A/Bb

3-17@ C: G#/Ab G: D#/Eb F: C#/Db Eb: B/Cb D: A#/Bb

3-19@ C: A#/Bb G: E#/F F: D#/Eb Eb: C#/Db A: G

3-25@

Too   many   Too few

ASSIGNMENT

Get a collection of George Gershwin, Jerome Kern or Irving Berlin songs out of the library, or buy one. Sing through as many of the songs as you can.

CHAPTER FOUR

MINOR SCALES

So far, we've only been working with the Major diatonic scale. But songs in minor keys use the minor diatonic scale. Fortunately, they're very similar.

Every Major key has a minor key related to it, called its relative minor. The scale of this key has the same notes as its relative Major, but it starts on the sixth note of the Major diatonic scale. So:

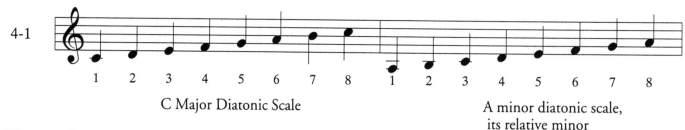

C Major Diatonic Scale

A minor diatonic scale, its relative minor

There are three versions of this minor scale:

1) the <u>Natural minor</u> (so named because it uses all the same notes as its relative Major, with no accidentals):

Sing it. Play it on the piano.

2) the <u>Harmonic minor</u> (because it has one accidental that's important to the harmony that often accompanies minor melodies):

Sing it. Play it.

3) the <u>Melodic minor</u> (because it has two accidentals which make it sound more like a melody than the Harmonic minor):

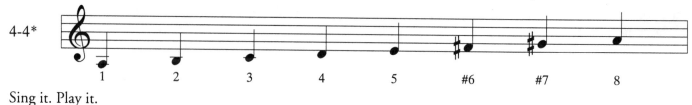

Sing it. Play it.

Music that's in a minor key will sometimes go back and forth between these three versions. But the important thing to note is that 1, 2, 3, 4, 5 and 8 of the three different versions are all the same; only 6 and 7 change.

We've had four other Major keys besides C Major. Start on 6 of each of them, sing the same notes that are in the Major diatonic scales, and you'll have the Natural version of those scales' relative minors:

4-5

G Major: G A B C D E F# G
E minor: E F# G A B C D E

F Major: F G A Bb C D E F
D minor: D E F G A Bb C D

Bb Major: Bb C D Eb F G A Bb
G minor: G A Bb C D Eb F G

Eb Major: Eb F G Ab Bb C D Eb
C minor: C D Eb F G Ab Bb C

Sing these Natural minor scales. Now, what are the Harmonic versions?

4-6@   E minor:

D minor:

G minor:

C minor:

Sing them. And finally, what are the Melodic versions?

4-7@   E minor:

D minor:

G minor:

C minor:

Sing them.

Since each Major diatonic scale and the Natural version of its relative minor have the same notes in them, they have the same key signature. For instance, Eb Major and C minor both have the same three flats in theirs. So how do we know if we're in a Major key or a minor key?

1) Look at the first chord of the song. The first chord of a song is usually made of the bells of the song's key. So if a song is in C Major, the first chord is usually the C chord, made up of C, E and G. If it's A minor, the first chord is usually the Amin chord (or Am or Ami), made up of A, C and E. Play these chords on the piano. Can you hear that one is Major and the other one is minor?
2) Look at the last note of the song. The last note of a song is almost always 1 or 8. If it's C, the song is probaly in C Major. If it's A, the song is almost certainly in A minor. But be careful: a lot of songs, particularly standards, start out in a minor key and end up in that key's relative Major. "My Funny Valentine" and "You'd Be So Nice To Come Home To" are two examples.
3) Listen to the harmony accompanying the melody. If the music sounds sad, dramatic, moody or angry, it's a good bet that it's in a minor key.

Once you've figured out that a song is in a minor key, sing 1, then 1 2 3 4 5 4 3 2 1, then the bells 1 3 5 8. Make sure the 3 is lower in pitch than the 3 in a Major diatonic scale. Get a good visual image of the scale and the bells on the staff.

Figuring out which 6 and which 7 to sing can be tricky. Think of it this way: there's a train track from 1 to 8, and after 5 it splits in two. The southern track has the natural notes on it (6 and 7). The northern track has the accidentals (#6 and #7). Then the tracks meet up again at 8.

Most often we'll sing the northern track, and when we do we'll see two accidentals in a row (a good tipoff that we're in a minor key). When you see these two accidentals in a row, think of the lead-in to the theme song for "The Addams Family" TV show:

That should help you to sing the #6 and #7, not 6 and 7. Try it.
Sing numbers, in any <u>minor</u> key that's comfortable:

4-9

1) 1	2	3	4	5	4	3	2	1	2	3	4	5	4	3	2	1
2) 1	3	5	8	5	3	1	3	5	8	5	3	1				
3) 1	2	3	4	5	6	7	8									
4) 1	2	3	4	5	6	#7	8									
5) 1	2	3	4	5	#6	#7	8									
6) 1	2	3	4	5	6	7	8	7	6	5	4	5	#6	#7	8	
7) 5	#6	#7	8	#7	#6	5										
	5	6	7	8	7	6	5	4	3	2	1					

MODULATIONS

Modulation means changing keys. Obviously, since this system of sightsinging is based on recognizing the notes of the key of the song, a new key could cause problems. There will be new notes in a new key. Adjustments need to be made.

There are two types of modulations:

1) the permanent kind, where we change keys for good, usually at the end of the song, and the key signature actually changes (once you hear the new key, forget the old one and sightsing as normal);
2) the temporary kind, which can happen at any time, and last anywhere from a half a measure to a whole section. There is no change in the key signature. So how do we know that we've changed keys?

First, we listen to the accompaniment. We'll feel that there is a new tonal center, a new set of bells, a new scale.

And second, we'll usually see an accidental or two in the melody. If we're in C Major and all of a suden we see a few F#s, we can guess that we've probably modulated to a key that has F# in it. G Major has one. In fact, F# is the only note in G Major that isn't in C Major. That's a good clue.

And if we're in C Major and we see a few Bbs, it's a good clue that we've gone to F Major. Bb is the only note in F Major that isn't in C Major.

So a modulation might look like this:

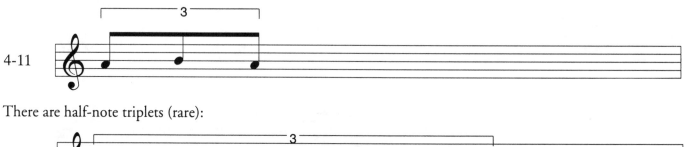

Do you see where the melody returns to C Major? If you sightsing or play this melody, can you hear the key change?

Note: once you've sung an accidental, get it out of your head. If you need to sing it again, you can find it again. But if it keeps you from hearing the note in the scale that it's replacing, you'll easily get lost.

TRIPLETS

The rhythms we've used so far all divide the measure equally (four quarter-notes in a measure of 4/4, two half-notes, etc.). But sometimes, composers want to divide a measure, or part of a measure, into thirds. Since there is no "one-third note", we use a "3" in a bracket to convey this rhythmic idea, and call the notes "triplets" (like "The Addams Family"):

There are half-note triplets (rare):

quarter-note triplets:

4-13

and eighth-note triplets:

4-14

All of these triplets take a space that is usually divided into two equal parts and divide it into three equal parts. All three of the triplet notes will last exactly the same amount of time. It helps when singing any triplet to emphasize each note, as if to say, "This isn't a mistake, I mean to sing it this way."

4-15

Which measures have too few or too many notes or rests?

4-16@

Sing along with the CD:

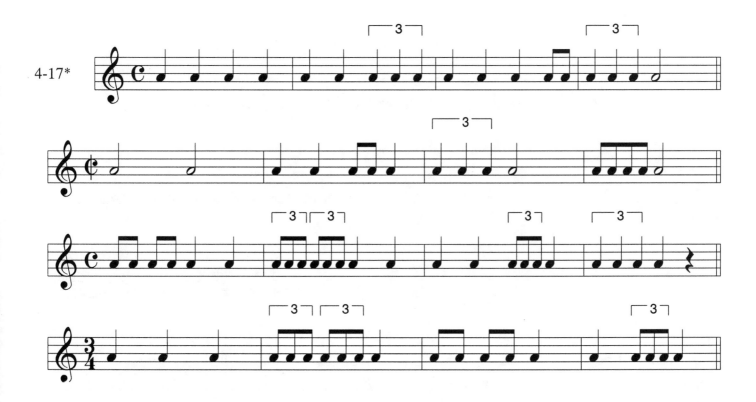

4-17*

BEGINNING SYNCOPATION

Syncopation is one of the hardest things about sightsinging. By now, it should be easy to sing quarter-notes and half-notes that line up with the beats "1 2 3 4" in each measure. Syncopation puts notes between those beats, on the "&s". We had a little bit of it in the last chapter, with ties.

There are eight eighth-notes in every measure of 4/4 (or cut time). Four are on numbers (beats), and four are on "&s":

If we accent the "&s" we have one simple kind of syncopation:

And if we tie an "&" to the next number, holding it over but not saying the next number, we have another kind of syncopation:

This is one of the things that makes modern music sound modern. Jazz, blues, pop, rock and R & B are all full of syncopation. If you see a lot of ties in your music, chances are good that there's a lot of syncopation.

Remember in Chapter Three when we introduced ties? We saw that there is a "technically correct" way of writing a rhythm, by writing out all the eighth-notes and tieing them together, and a way that's "technically incorrect", that makes two tied eighth notes into a quarter-note. You'll see this "technically incorrect" way of writing a lot. Half of the examples and exercises will be written this way.

Although syncopation is hard to read until you practice it a lot, you hear it so much in so many styles of music that it will be easy to sing once you read it correctly. Keep your ears open while you're sightsinging. If you hear it correctly a few times, yxou'll memorize it correctly.

Sing along with the CD:

EXAMPLES

A*   1 C   2 D   3 E   4 F   5 G   5 G   5 G   4 F   3 E   3 E   3 E   2 D   2 D   1 C   1 C

EXERCISES

58

This page has been intentionally left blank.

SONG 4*

Slow, moody ballad

Those af-ter-noons, sit-ting all a-lone, no-one but me I still re-mem-ber lone-li-er days, that's how it used to be. Those som-ber hours walk-ing by my-self, no com-pa-ny I still re-mem-ber lone-li-er nights, that's how it used to be. Then you came a-long and made right out of wrong clear bright blue skies out of gray. You made all of the heart-ache dis-ap-pear, love can be fun-ny that way.

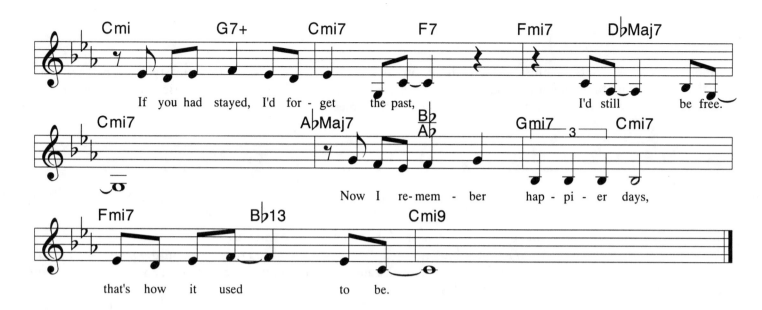

ANSWERS

4-6@ E minor: E F# G A B C D# E

D minor: D E F G A Bb C# D

G minor: G A Bb C D Eb F# G

C minor: C D Eb F G Ab B C

4-7@ E minor: E F# G A B C# D# E

D minor: D E F G A B C# D

G minor: G A Bb C D E F# G

C minor: C D Eb F G A B C

Too Many   Too Few

ASSIGNMENT

Get a book out of the library, or buy one, of early rock 'n roll (Elvis Presley, Buddy Holly) or '60s or '70s pop-rock (Carole King, Simon and Garfunkel). Read through as many of the songs as you can. If you already know them, be careful to sing them exactly as they're written, not as you remember them from the record.

CHAPTER FIVE

THE BLUES SCALE

Almost every kind of popular music in the 20th Century is based on the blues: jazz in its many styles, gospel, rhythm and blues, rock and roll, soul, funk and pop. It's the notes in the blues scale that all of these kinds of music have in common. You've heard these notes many times, and undoubtedly sung them many times:

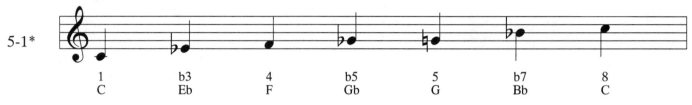

5-1*

1	b3	4	b5	5	b7	8
C	Eb	F	Gb	G	Bb	C

Sing this scale up and down until you know it by heart. Often you'll sing 2 and 6 as well.

The three flat notes (b3, b5 and b7) are the blue notes. Strictly speaking, blue notes aren't on the piano, they're in the cracks between notes. They can only be made by the human voice and by instruments that can slide up and down. This sliding, or "bending", is one of the things that makes the blues so emotional.

So when we sing blue notes, we try not to sing them precisely, like we sing other notes. Their pitch is a little lower than the notes on the piano. To convey this idea, composers may use dynamic markings like these:

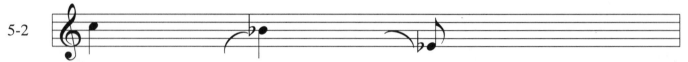

5-2

to indicate that they want us to bend blue notes. Or they may simply write a description at the top of the page ("Bluesy") and leave the rest to us.

Although b3, b5 and b7 are going to sound a lot like the accidentals we learned to hear in Chapter Three, let's try to find a new way of hearing them as blue notes. Maybe they're train whistles in the night.

The first blue note, b3, is the most dissonant (that is, it "rubs" against the accompanying chord, it doesn't "fit in", it conflicts). You'll often hear it while that chord made of bells is accompanying it:

5-3*

b3

Play the chord while singing the note. Hear the dissonance, the "rub"? That's another one of the things that makes the blues so emotional.

b3 is probably the most-often used blue note. Whether it fits into the chord in the accompaniment or not, you can sing it and hang on to it for a long time, shake it, bend it, growl it. Eventually, usually, it falls down to 1, and the phrase is over. Sometimes it uses 2 to get to 1.

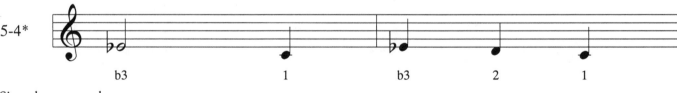

5-4*

b3	1	b3	2	1

Sing these two phrases.

Think of b3 as a freight train with a lonesome traveler on it.

The next most important blue note is b7. You can hang on to b7 for a long time, too, bend it and shout it, over any chord in the blues. It usually falls down to 5, sometimes using 6 to get there.

5-5*

b7	5	b7	6	5

Sing these two phrases.

But b7 can go up to 8, too.

5-6*

b7   8

Sing this phrase.

Think of b7 as a long-distance passenger train with a broken-hearted rider on it.

And lastly, b5 is the blue note that we don't hold on to for very long. It's a passing note, and we usually hear it resolve quickly to 4 and then to b3:

5-7*

b5   4   b3

Sing it.

Sometimes b5 will bend all the way up to 5:

5-8*

b5   5

Sing it.

Think of b5 as an express train rushing by.

The great thing about the blues is that you can sing any note in the blues scale over any of the various chords used to accompany you, whether it's in the chords or not, and it will sound OK, as long as you sing it with conviction. That's why the blues, a very simple form with simple chords and simple notes, has been so influential in the last 100 years: it's easy, it's fun and it's emotional. And there are endless variations. That's why there's so much improvisation in the blues, and why it gave rise to jazz, which is all about improvisation. Later it gave rise to rhythm and blues and rock and roll. These styles of music may not have as much improvisation as jazz does, but listen to the improvised guitar and organ and saxophone and piano solos; they're almost always based on the blues scale.

What are b3, b5 and b7 in the following keys?:

5-9@   G:

F:

Bb:

Eb:

Sing numbers in any key:

5-10   1) 1   b3   4   b5   5   b7   8   b7   5   b5   4   b3   1

2) 1   b3   1   4   1   b5   1   5   1   b7   1   8

3) 1   2   b3   4   b5   4   b3   1

4) 8   b7   8   b7   8   b7   5   b7   6   5   b7   8

5) b5   4   b3   1   b5   4   b3   1   b5   4   b3   1

JAZZ EIGHTHS

The other hallmark of jazz, besides improvisation, is swing. Swing is hard to define, but it's mostly a rhythmic "bounce". That bounce is provided by jazz eighths.

Regular eighth-notes are all equal in duration:

If we make the first eighth of each pair a little longer (with a dot) and the second eighth of each pair a little shorter (with a flag) we have jazz eighths that bounce, and swing:

or

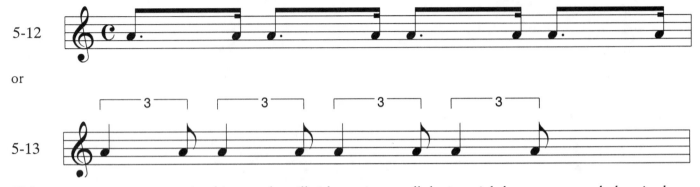

If the composer want us to swing his song, he will either write out all the jazz eighths, or put a symbol up in the top left hand corner of the music above the first staff, to indicate what he wants:

or

5-15

This means "whenever you see straight eighths, sing them as jazz eighths, swing them." Jazz eighths can be easy to sing once you recognize the pattern. They are not necessarily syncopated.

Sing along with the CD:

ADVANCED SYNCOPATION

In the last chapter, we introduced syncopation with eighth notes. More advanced syncopation has sixteenth-notes, and to sing it, you have to count very carefully, and start memorizing patterns. If you can recognize a pattern, you won't have to count it out every time.

We'll be using the following patterns:

Remember: just because there are dots and flags, it doesn't mean a rhythm is necessarily syncopated. The following pattern swings (it's jazz eighths) but it's not syncopated:

Look for ties. Syncopation is about singing a note earlier or later in the measure than you might expect, "kicking" it off a number:

The first step in reading a heavily syncopated rhythm is to divide the measure into four equal pieces. Each piece will get a number (the beats 1,2,3,4), and will equal a quarter note:

If you can see where the numbers are in each measure (the beginning of each piece), you'll group the notes into manageable units (5-17), and sing them in the right places.

Put numbers in the right places:

The next step is to sing each of the units at the right time in the measure. For this, we may need to start counting eighth-notes instead of quarter-notes:

Now some of the sixteenth-notes will be off the beat, like the eighth-notes were in Chapter Four.

The next step is to connect notes that are tied. You may need to really slow down the tempo for a while. But keep your ears open, memorize the rhythm correctly and then start speeding up the tempo.

Once you've got it, go back to counting just quarter-notes (stop counting the eighth-notes in between).

The last step is to go from measure to measure. Sometimes a note at the end of a bar will be tied to the first note of the next bar:

Or several measures in a row will have advanced syncopation:

Don't stop to congratulate yourself because you've sung one measure correctly. The music will go on without you. When singing from measure to measure, listen carefully for downbeats. Slap your thigh a little louder on "1" of each measure.

A few more words of advice:

1) If you make a mistake, keep going, and go back later to correct it.
2) Don't get so caught up in syncopation that you can't sing an easier rhythm. Once you start syncopating, it's hard to stop.
3) Try to sing the lyric as soon as possible. It will usually help you with the rhythm. Complicated rhythm is usually complicated for a reason: it fits the lyric. Usually it enables the singer to sing a phrase the way she would say it, not in a sing-song, even way (four quarter-notes to the measure) but more conversationally.
4) There's a square way to sing and a hip way to sing. Syncopation is the hip way. Compare the following two rhythms:

Which sounds hipper? It's harder to read, but it should be easier to sing, eventually. If you keep your ears open, kick notes, use your instincts as well as your eyes, you'll hear it.

Sing along with the CD:

5-27*

EXAMPLES

Note:
1. All accidentals have two names, one sharp and one flat;
   A = Bb, etc.
2. Flatting a note that is already flat will produce a double flat; flatting Bb = Bbb, etc.

L*

M*

N*

O*

P*

Q*

R*

S*

T*

EXERCISES

19

20
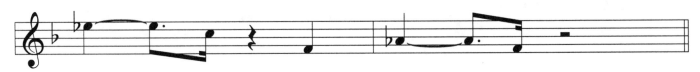

21

22

23

24

25

26

27

SONG 5*

Bluesy, with jazz eighths

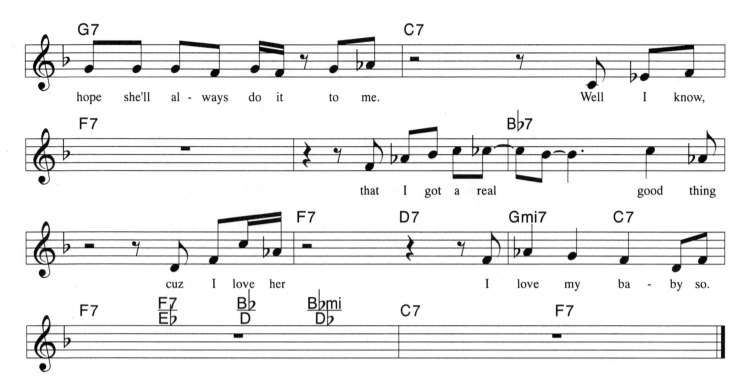

hope she'll al - ways do it to me. Well I know,

that I got a real good thing

cuz I love her I love my ba - by so.

ANSWERS

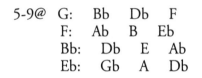

5-9@ G: Bb Db F
F: Ab B Eb
Bb: Db E Ab
Eb: Gb A Db

ASSIGNMENT

Get out of the library (or buy) a book of '50s and '60s rhythm and blues for blue notes (BB King, Chuck Berry); and '60s Motown for syncopation (Marvin Gaye, Stevie Wonder) and make sure that all the syncopation is written out, the way the singer sang it, with lots of ties and sixteenth-notes.

APPENDIX
STEPS TO SIGHTSINGING

1) Determine the key from the key signature and sing the diatonic scale in that key. This scale is our best friend. Sing it until you're confidently in that key, singing the notes you'll use most often. Find the scale on the staff - get a good visual image of it, as though it's in brackets.

2) Find the starting pitch. Hold onto it - it's easy to get confused and start on the wrong note.

3) Figure out the meter from the time signature, and start your internal metronome; clap your hands, snap your fingers, tap your foot, slap your thigh, anything that ends in "ap" to help you feel the meter consistently. Take it at your own, slow tempo, and speed up later if necessary.

4) Associate the note on the staff with its number in the scale: that will help you find its pitch. The sound of each number in relation to its key has a character to it, a feel, an emotional quality, that will stay the same from key to key (3 will sound like 3 in any key). And turn off the "melody-maker" in your head that thinks it already knows what the notes are.

5) Sing through the song slowly on numbers. Tie each note on the staff to its number and then sing the sound of that number (its pitch). Get the notes first, then the rhythms, and then the lyrics. But try to get to the lyrics as quickly as you can, because they will usually help you with the rhythms.

6) MOST IMPORTANTLY: Keep your ears open! The goal of sightsinging is to memorize the music, so you don't have to sightsing it again. It may take a few times through - get as much of it as you can each time. If you concentrate all your energy through your eyes, you won't hear what you're singing, so you won't be able to repeat it, with words and dynamics and expressiveness. Listen to yourself sing, and memorize as quickly as possible.

Here's a key to memorization: music loves patterns. Songwriters write melodic patterns so that their melodies are more easily recognized, more singable, more memorable. Without patterns, melodies would be totally random and they wouldn't burrow their way into our heads. Separate the melody into sections, and see and hear where the patterns repeat.